D1175543

Sbjc

NURSES

BY EMMA LESS

AMICUS READERS ● AMICUS INK

Amicus Readers and Amicus Ink are imprints of Amicus
P.O. Box 1329, Mankato, MN 56002
www.amicuspublishing.us

Cataloging-in-Publication Data is on file with the Library of Congress.
ISBN 978-1-68151-297-6 (library binding)
ISBN 978-1-68152-279-1 (paperback)
ISBN 978-1-68151-359-1 (eBook)

Editor: Valerie Bodden
Designer: Patty Kelley

Photo Credits:
Cover: Monkey Business Images/Dreamstime.com
Inside: Adobe Stock: Bst2012 10, Dreamstime.com: Sergii Chalenko 3, Wavebreakmedia Ltd 6, Monkey Business Images 8, Michael Zhang 12, Steve Heap 16L, Robert Radelowski 16R, Thodonal 16B, Shutterstock: Monkey Business Images H

Printed in China.

HC 10 9 8 7 6 5 4 3 2 1
PB 10 9 8 7 6 5 4 3 2 1

Some kids get sick. They go
to the hospital. Nurses help them.

The nurse asks
Anna how she feels.
She helps
her into bed.

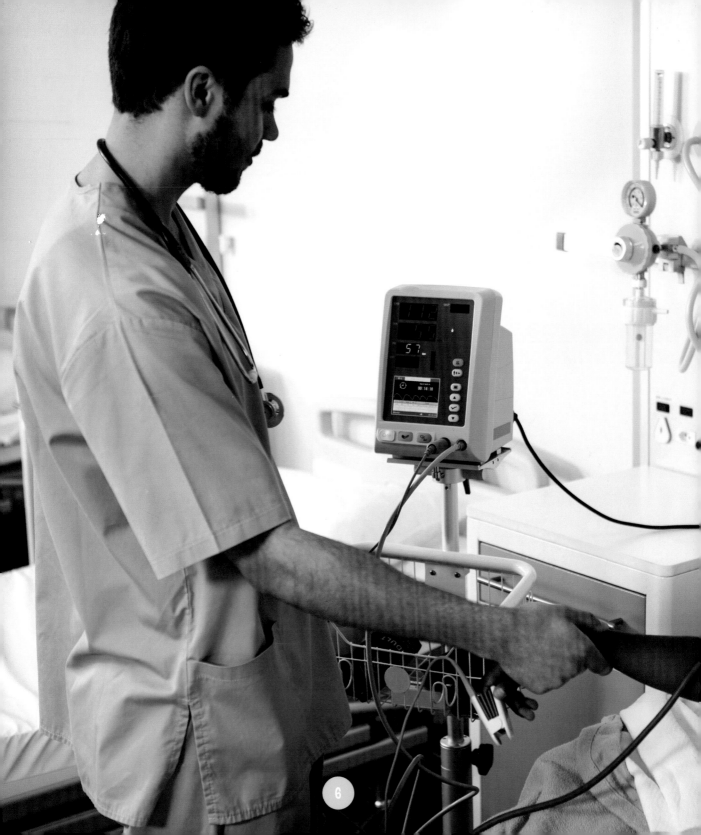

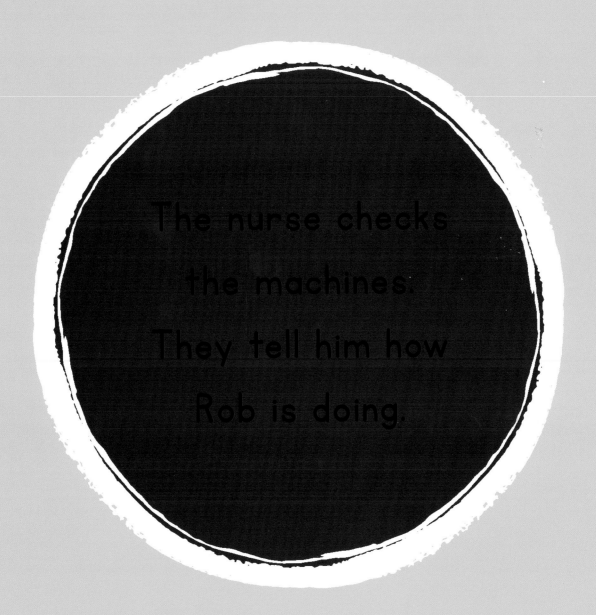

The nurse checks
the machines.
They tell him how
Rob is doing.

Time to eat!
The nurse brings
Carlos lunch.

Andy needs a shot.
The nurse is gentle.

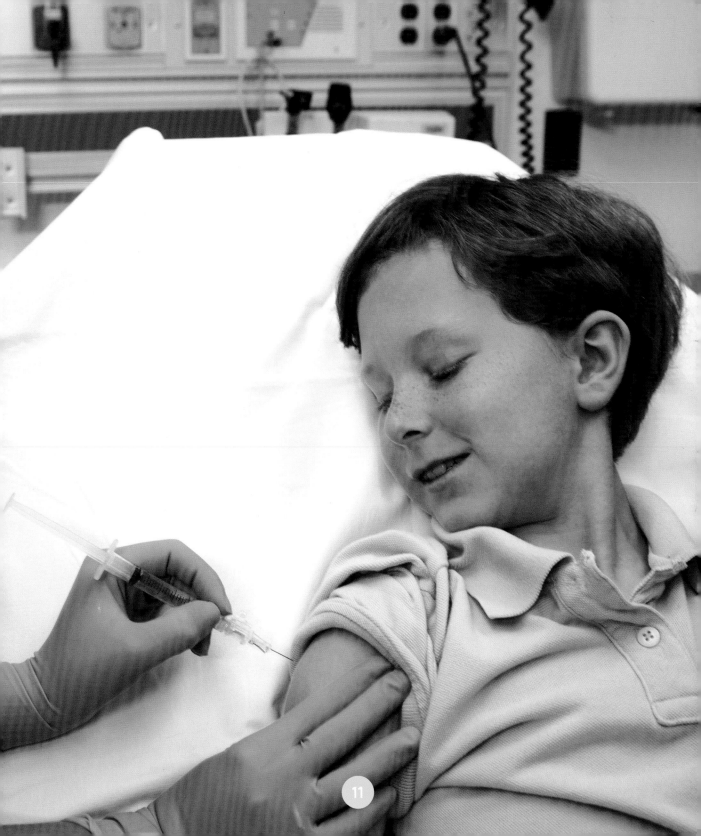

13

Nurses help us
feel better.
Thank you, nurse!

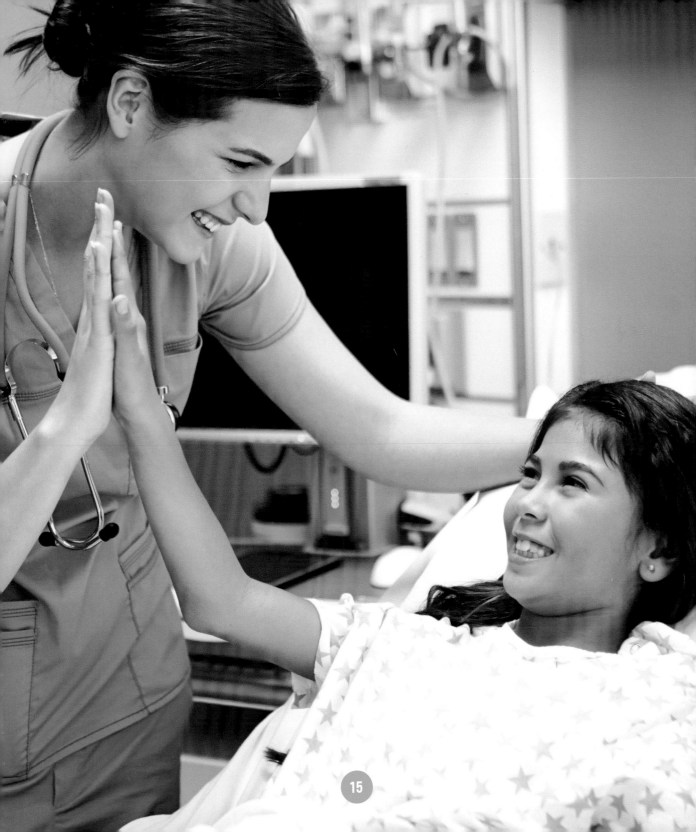

SEEN WITH A NURSE

scrubs

thermometer

bandages